W9-ACW-495

Adopted

Judith E. Greenberg
and Helen H. Carey

photographs by
Barbara Kirk

JOSEPH VILE MEMORIAL LIBRARY
Rt. 6, Box 16
Pound Ridge, New York
10576

Franklin Watts/New York
London/Toronto/Sydney/1987

2.64

9.40

WLS

5188

J
362.7
G

51795

Library of Congress Cataloging-in-Publication Data

Greenberg, Judith E.
Adopted.

(My World)
Summary: Because both Sarah and her new brother are
adopted, Sarah's mother, father, and grandfather
explain what adoption and being part of a family
are all about.
1. Adoption—Juvenile literature. [1. Adoption.
2. Family life] I. Carey, Helen H. II. Kirk,
Barbara, ill. III. Title. IV. Series: My world
(Franklin Watts, inc.)
HV875.G736 1987   362.7'34   87-6189
ISBN 0-531-10290-4

Text copyright © 1987 by Judith E. Greenberg
and Helen H. Carey
Photographs copyright © 1987 by Franklin Watts, Inc.
All rights reserved
Printed in the United States of America
5   4   3   2   1

For Mitchell and Wendy,
I love you

J. G.

For Evan and Ryan

H. C.

Sarah and Ryan are both adopted. Their adoptive parents wanted children very much and they adopted Sarah seven years ago. Ryan was adopted last week. Now there are four people in Sarah's family.

Sarah likes being Ryan's big sister. Being a big sister is an important job. She tries to be quiet when Ryan takes a nap, and answers the phone when her mother gives Ryan his bottle. Her favorite job is taking pictures of Ryan with her new camera. She also takes pictures of the people who come to visit their new baby.

Today, Sarah's best friend, Ann, came to see Ryan and play with Sarah. Sarah took a picture of Ann holding Ryan.

Sarah and Ann like to ride bikes together. Sometimes they have special talks about their families, friends, and school.

Ann asked Sarah if adopted babies could be taken back if they cried too much. She told Sarah that her brother cried so much that once she wished her mom would take him back to the hospital.

"Nobody can send Ryan back," said Sarah. "We adopted him and he's part of our family now."

"Why didn't your mom go to the hospital to get the baby like my mom did?" asked Ann.

Sarah's mother heard Ann and stopped to answer her question. She explained that sometimes a healthy baby can't grow in a mother's uterus.

"The uterus is the part of a woman's body where the baby grows for nine months until it is ready to be born. Sarah and Ryan were born in a hospital but I wasn't there. I didn't see Sarah or Ryan until we went to the adoption agency to get them."

Turning to Sarah, she said, "Your dad and I saw you and loved you right away."

That night, when Sarah's mom was reading to her, Sarah asked who her real mother was. "I am. I'm Ryan's mother, too," her mom answered. "I didn't help you to be born, but I am your mother because I take care of you and love you."

Sarah thought of another question she wanted to ask. "How did I get born?"

"You were born in a hospital," her mother said. "I do not know the name of the woman who was your birth-parent. She was able to have a baby grow in her uterus but maybe wasn't ready to be a mother. Maybe she was all alone or too young, but she was a good person. She let you be adopted so you could have all the things you need to grow up happy and healthy."

"Your mom is right," Sarah's dad said as he sat down on the bed. "Mothers and fathers have to work hard to take care of their children. In our family, Mom and I take turns giving Ryan his nighttime bottle. We take you to the doctor when you get sick and make sure you eat good food and get enough sleep."

The next day Grandpa and Aunt Kate came to see the new baby. Sarah took lots of pictures of Grandpa, Aunt Kate, and Ryan.

Sarah and Grandpa looked at the pictures of her family. Her mother is short and her dad is tall. Aunt Kate has blue eyes and Grandpa has brown eyes. Ryan has curly blond hair and Sarah has straight hair.

"Who do I look like, Grandpa?" asked Sarah.

"Sometimes you walk like your mom, or smile like your dad, but you will always look like you." said Grandpa, hugging her tightly.

Sarah has two friends who were adopted. Long Suciu is from Vietnam and came to live with his American family when he was six years old. Everyone in Sarah's class is helping Long Suciu to learn English. Long Suciu showed the class where his country is on a map and told them about his trip in an airplane.

Brian is also adopted. He lives near Sarah's grandpa's house. Sarah and Brian have snowball fights when Sarah spends winter vacation with her grandpa. One day some big kids teased Sarah and Brian about being adopted. Sarah started to cry.

Grandpa hugged Sarah and told her that being adopted is just another way to become part of a family.

"Being adopted doesn't make you different or special. You are special because you are Sarah."

"You are special because you
are nice to your brother . . .

care about people's feelings . . .

remember your dad
on Father's Day . . .

help your mom make bread . . .

share your playthings with
your friends. . . . ''

"You are special because . . .

your family loves you.''